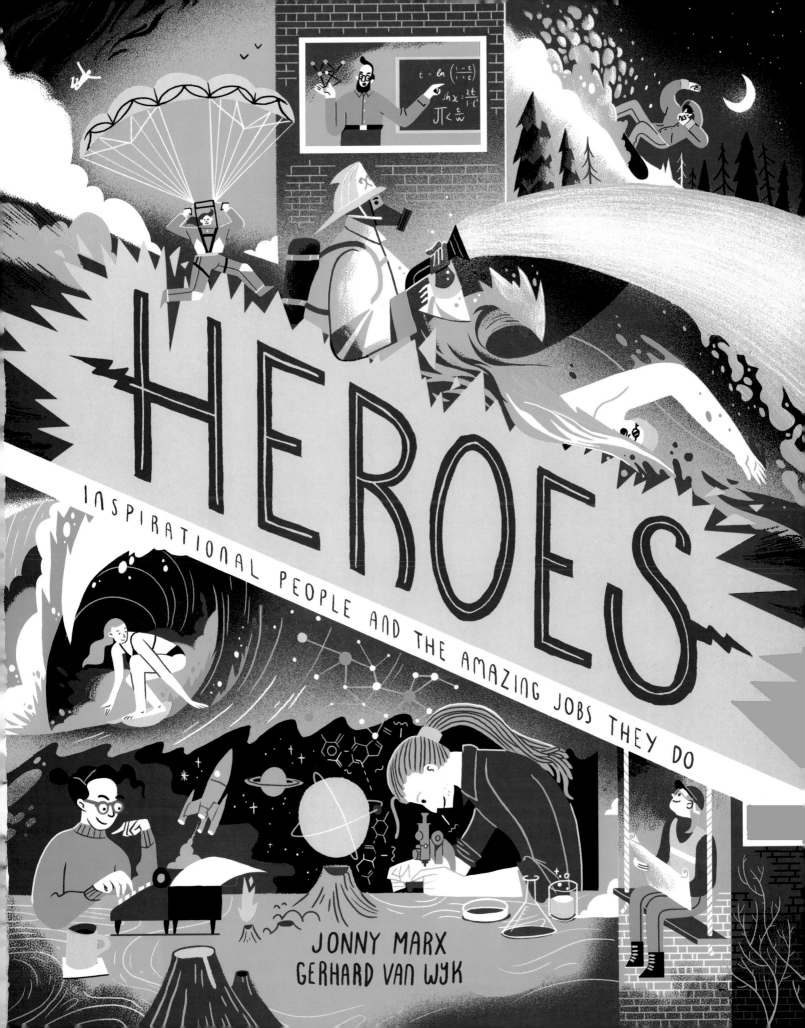

WRITTEN by
JONNY MARX

ILLUSTRATED by
GERHARD VAN WYK

The world is an ever-changing place and
the people within it are capable of incredible
things; discoveries are made, records are broken,
new facts are found and history recovered.
We will be happy to revise and update
information in future editions.

ABOUT
THE ARTIST

Gerhard Van Wyk is an illustrator and graphic
designer. He lives in Cape Town, South Africa.
When not swimming in cold water, he can be
found climbing rocks on the Cape Peninsula.

360 DEGREES
An imprint of the Little Tiger Group
1 Coda Studios, 189 Munster Road, London SW6 6AW
www.littletiger.co.uk
First published in Great Britain 2019
Text by Jonny Marx
Text copyright © 2019 Caterpillar Books Ltd
Illustrations copyright © 2019 Gerhard Van Wyk
A CIP catalogue record for this book is available from the British Library
All rights reserved
Printed in China
ISBN: 978-1-84857-873-9
CPB/1800/1097/0319
10 9 8 7 6 5 4 3 2 1

INTRODUCTION

If you're not quite sure whether superheroes really exist, look no further . . .

This book showcases the incredible achievements and heroic endeavours of real-life people, their professions, passions and their pursuits.

From firefighters, police officers and vets, to conservationists, big-wave surfers, mountain climbers and more, the people in this book prove that not all heroes wear capes – though some do have colourful costumes and magnificent masks! Some have superior strength, amazing agility and unrivalled dedication, while others have unbridled bravery and the brains to match! You may even discover your dream job along the way.

CONTENTS

So what are you waiting for? It's time to forget Batman, Spiderman and Wonder Woman and focus on the heroics that happen in the REAL WORLD.

EXPLORERS

The golden age of exploration may have been and gone, but that hasn't stopped the world's intrepid explorers. There are still unconquered mountains to climb, areas of the ocean that have never been dived, round-the-world records to break and new species to discover.

Explorers tend to be inquisitive, extremely determined and physically fit. Whether it be sailing, climbing, trekking, diving or spacewalking, adventurers are usually well-versed in survival techniques and training.

And they're not deterred by failure! Even world-famous climber Conrad Anker was not perturbed by defeat when trying to climb Meru Peak in India. It took him three attempts to become the first to climb the mountain.

THE ARCTIC

Both Frederick Cook and Robert Peary claimed to have been the first to reach the North Pole during their lifetimes. However, no one is quite sure which man was telling the truth and the evidence remains disputed.

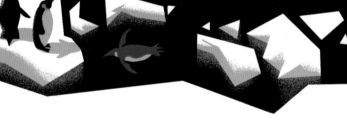

THE SOUTH POLE

Norwegian explorer Roald Amundsen and his trekking team were the first to reach the South Pole. They managed to navigate the colossal glaciers, ice-swept plains and cope with sub-zero temperatures, reaching the pole on 14th December, 1911.

The Norwegian team beat another expedition led by British naval officer turned adventurer, Robert Falcon Scott. Scott's team arrived at the site a month after the Norwegians and, realising that they had lost the race to reach the pole, began an arduous 800-mile journey back north. On the way, however, disaster struck! The dejected men lost their bearings in the Antarctic wilderness and fell victim to plummeting temperatures and dwindling food rations. Sadly, Scott's team perished on the Antarctic ice, only to be discovered almost eight months later by another expedition.

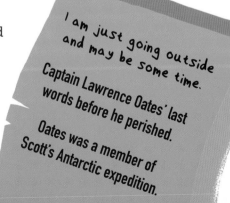

I am just going outside and may be some time.

Captain Lawrence Oates' last words before he perished.

Oates was a member of Scott's Antarctic expedition.

Sacagawea was a Native American from the Shoshone tribe.

SACAGAWEA

In the early 1800s, Sacagawea played a vital role in assisting a colossal expedition across America, spanning thousands of miles.

The journey, which began in the state of Missouri, was led by military personnel Meriwether Lewis and William Clark, and took approximately two years to complete. It is thought that Sacagawea acted as a translator for certain legs of the trek, conversing with tribes along the way, and that she helped guide the company using her knowledge of flora and fauna. Amazingly, Sacagawea completed the majority of the expedition with her newborn baby in tow!

NORTH AMERICA

Long before Christopher Columbus 'discovered' the Americas, the Vikings landed on Canadian shores but were fought off by natives and forced from the continent.

LAURA DEKKER

Laura Dekker became the youngest person to sail solo around the world when she arrived at the Caribbean island of Sint Maarten in 2012. The odyssey took 518 days to complete and Laura was just 16 years old when she landed ashore.

SOUTH AMERICA

Spanish explorer Hernán Cortés sailed to Mexico in the 16th Century. His men brought with them many foreign illnesses and diseases, wiping out a large portion of the Mexican population and causing the Aztec civilization to collapse.

JAMES COOK

Captain James Cook was the finest explorer and naval commander of the 18th century. He travelled thousands of miles across the seas and explored more foreign lands and waters than any other globetrotter of his generation.

INTO THIN AIR

Mount Everest soars 8,848m (29,029ft) into the sky and is the tallest mountain above sea level in the world. It is one of the most dangerous peaks to climb because of its altitude (height above sea level).

Tenzing Norgay and Edmund Hillary were the first people to climb Everest. Their 1953 expedition took months to plan and required more than 370 people (including 20 Sherpas and 350 porters) and tonnes of equipment and supplies.

Their victory was momentous, proving for the first time that humans could travel to any terrestrial height! Nowadays, Everest is climbed by hundreds of people every year.

If you were to teleport directly to Everest's summit, you would only survive for a few minutes because your body wouldn't have had time to get used to the altitude.

THE DEATH ZONE

The most dangerous area on a big mountain is nicknamed 'The Death Zone'. This area refers to anywhere above 8,000m (26,247ft). Oxygen levels are so thin at these heights that most climbers have to take oxygen canisters with them. Even Tenzing Norgay and Edmund Hillary took oxygen canisters on their onerous journey.

DID YOU KNOW?
Jordan Romero became the youngest person to climb Everest in 2010. He was just 13 years old at the time.

SHERPAS
Most of the Sherpa people live in mountainous regions of Nepal, China, India and Bhutan. Their unparalleled ability to cope with conditions at altitude, and expert knowledge of mountains and mountain survival make them invaluable to many expeditions in the Himalayas.

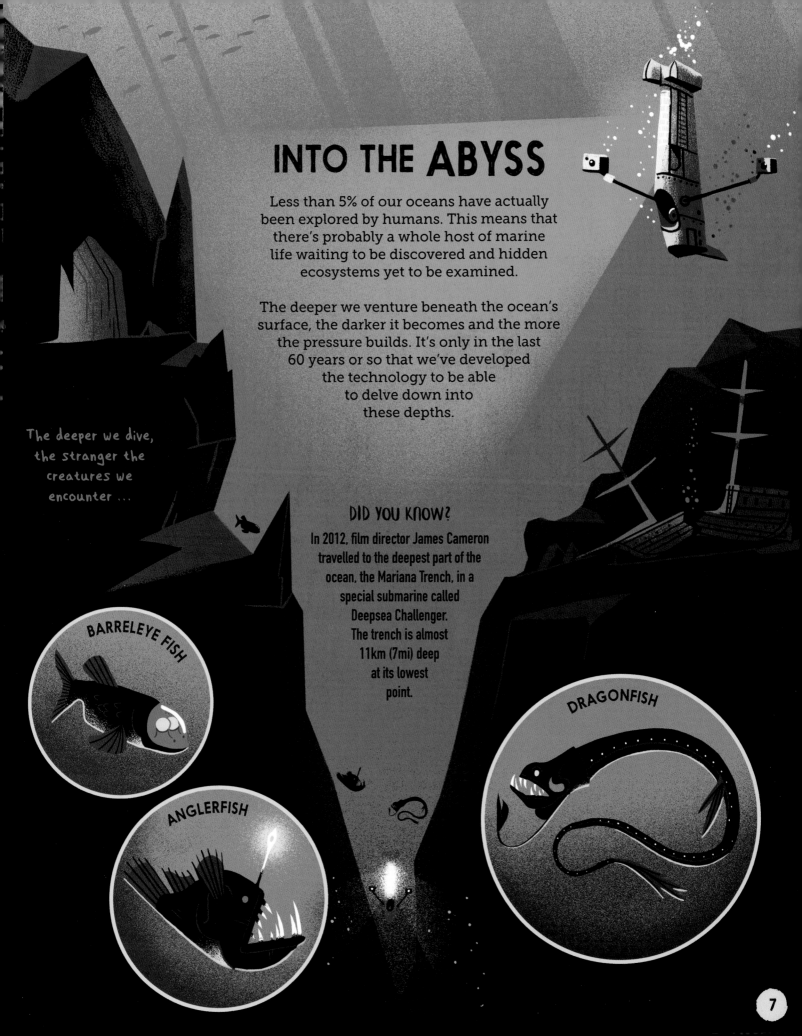

INTO THE ABYSS

Less than 5% of our oceans have actually been explored by humans. This means that there's probably a whole host of marine life waiting to be discovered and hidden ecosystems yet to be examined.

The deeper we venture beneath the ocean's surface, the darker it becomes and the more the pressure builds. It's only in the last 60 years or so that we've developed the technology to be able to delve down into these depths.

The deeper we dive, the stranger the creatures we encounter ...

DID YOU KNOW?

In 2012, film director James Cameron travelled to the deepest part of the ocean, the Mariana Trench, in a special submarine called Deepsea Challenger. The trench is almost 11km (7mi) deep at its lowest point.

BARRELEYE FISH

ANGLERFISH

DRAGONFISH

ALBERT I
FIRST ASTRONAUT
Albert I was a rhesus monkey. He rode a V-2 rocket more than 30 miles into the sky in 1948.

INTO THE BEYOND
Though we may have explored most of what planet Earth has to offer, space is a completely different story. We've still not even made it to Mars, let alone to other solar systems or galaxies!

NEIL ARMSTRONG
FIRST PERSON ON THE MOON
In 1969, Neil Armstrong became the first person to walk on the Moon, followed closely by Buzz Aldrin.

LAIKA
FIRST ANIMAL TO ORBIT EARTH
This Soviet space dog travelled aboard the Sputnik II satellite in 1957.

WHO?
FIRST PERSON ON MARS
NASA believes humankind will land on Mars within the next 30 years.

YURI GAGARIN
FIRST PERSON IN SPACE
Yuri Gagarin travelled into space on his Vostok 1 craft. He completed an orbit of Earth before re-entering its atmosphere, landing safely back in Russia on April 12th, 1961.

VALENTINA TERESHKOVA
FIRST WOMAN IN SPACE
Valentina volunteered for the Vostok 6 space mission, which launched on 16th June, 1963.

By looking through powerful telescopes, astronomers have been able to discover some astonishing things in space, including stars orbiting stars, black holes (areas in space where the force of gravity is so strong that even light can't escape), quasars (the brightest things in the known universe), comets, meteors and much more!

PHYSICISTS

Physicists help research and explain the governing forces around us, and the ways in which these forces work and interact with one another.

Physicists can be involved in all sorts of industries, from aeronautical travel and exploration to automobile efficiency. Physicists are even required in fields and areas you might not expect, such as helping designers engineer forces and physical principals in video games or making sure a computer character moves and jumps in a realistic way.

Physicists have an innate understanding of mathematics, equations and forces, and are inquisitive about the particles and building blocks that combine to make the world work.

There are plenty of different types of physicists and most specialise in a particular area of interest. Theoretical physicists (Albert Einstein and Stephen Hawking, for example) use mathematics and formulae to help make sense of the world around us.

$$P = \frac{mv}{\sqrt{1 - \frac{v^2}{a}}}$$

$$E = mc^2$$

$$h\nu = A + \frac{1}{2}\frac{2}{2}$$

$$R_x = \frac{35}{8}$$

$$\lambda = \frac{h}{p}$$

$$PE = Mgh$$

$$P = P_e$$

$$E_cB = \triangle mc^2$$

DID YOU KNOW?
When she was just 11 years old, Kashmea Wahi
scored 162 (the perfect score) in a MENSA IQ
test, beating Einstein's estimated score of 160!

ALBERT EINSTEIN

Albert Einstein's unparalleled understanding
of mathematics and physics made him one of
the brightest sparks the world has ever seen.

Born in Ulm, Germany, in 1879, he won a Nobel Prize
in 1921 for his groundbreaking research focussing on
light and electricity. He gave us the famous equation ...

$$E=mc^2$$

... explaining how atomic energy works, why the Sun and
stars shine and why atomic bombs explode. His Theory
of Relativity helped us understand the possibilities of
space travel and he taught us that gravity warps space
itself, causing it to curve (in the way a trampoline would
bend if we were to roll a bowling ball into its centre).

Einstein lived during a turbulent time in world history
and he fled Germany for America before the outbreak
of World War II. As a Jewish scientist, he saw the
dangers attributed to living under Nazi rule and
helped facilitate the escape of many other
scientists from Nazi-occupied countries.

DID YOU KNOW?
After his death in 1955, Albert's brain was
so sought after in the scientific world that it was
removed from his body by his doctor and kept in a jar.

STEPHEN HAWKING

Despite being diagnosed with Motor Neurone Disease at the age of 21, Stephen Hawking lived to the ripe old age of 76 and led a life full of scientific discovery. His research into black holes took the scientific world by storm and his 1988 book, *A Brief History Of Time*, made him a household name, selling more than ten million copies (... and counting). Hawking was also famed for his wry sense of humour and he notoriously zoomed around Cambridge on his mobility scooter, aiming for students' toes!

'My goal is simple. It is a complete understanding of the universe, why it is as it is and why it exists at all.'

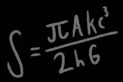

$$S = \frac{\pi A k c^3}{2 \hbar G}$$

BLACK HOLES

Black holes suck all sorts of matter towards them because they possess an enormous gravitational force. Towards the edge of a black hole exists an area known as an 'event horizon', a point of no return from which nothing (not even light) can escape. Despite its name, a black hole isn't actually a hole, but a sphere of incredibly dense matter, often created as a dying star implodes.

ISAAC NEWTON

$$F = G\frac{m_1 m_2}{r^2}$$

Isaac Newton's mother wanted him to follow in his father's footsteps by becoming a farmer, but Isaac's mind was set on bigger things! According to the famous story, Isaac was sitting under an apple tree when he noticed one of the fruits fall from a branch. Pondering why the apple fell down, rather than sideways, he began to develop his laws of gravity.

Isaac went on to write many scientific papers, outlining his understanding of motion, gravity, light and even a new form of mathematics now referred to as calculus.

CHEMISTS

Chemists look at the structures and properties of chemical elements to create different compounds and mixtures. Their findings and discoveries can be used across all industries.

Whether it be the creation of a biodegradable plastic, a biofuel to power our cars, a new medicine or the discovery of a new element, chemistry affects our world – even the clothing we wear may be made from synthetic fibres that chemists constructed, and the pavement we walk on could be produced from the combination of chemical elements.

Just like physicists, many chemists explore their field through the wonderful world of academia by studying Chemistry at school, university and in labs and research facilities.

DID YOU KNOW?
Marie Curie was so iconic that the element Curium was named in her honour.

DID YOU KNOW?
Radioactive isotopes have a half-life, indicating how long it takes them to lose half of their power or potency. It can take some radioactive particles millions, if not billions, of years to diminish or decay. Caffeine, a drug which can be found in things like fizzy drinks and coffee, is radioactive, though its half-life is just 5-6 hours.

MARIE CURIE

Marie Skłodowska Curie is famous for her research into radioactivity, a term which she herself coined. She won not one, but two Nobel prizes for her endeavours, and is still the only person to have won the award across two sciences (Physics and Chemistry).

Marie, and her husband Pierre, worked with radioactive chemical elements including polonium and radium. These elements are so harmful, in fact, that they made Marie quite sick and some of the equipment and books that the dynamic duo used are still highly radioactive and will remain so for hundreds of years!

ROSALIND FRANKLIN

During her short lifetime, Rosalind Franklin discovered the unusual structure of DNA, paving the way for James Watson and Francis Crick to identify it as a double helix (two spirals joined together). Franklin conducted her research using X-rays, which may have contributed to the cause of her untimely death in 1958. We now know that over-exposure to radiation from X-rays is harmful. Franklin also investigated the structure of viruses during her career, leaving a legacy that ultimately helped virologists discover cures.

ALFRED NOBEL
Alfred Nobel was a chemist, engineer and inventor. He is credited with creating dynamite and he patented more than 300 other compounds, inventions and methods. He used the wealth amassed during his lifetime to fund the Nobel Prizes.

DNA DOUBLE HELIX

PERPLEXING PLASTIC
In 2018, scientists created an enzyme capable of breaking down plastic by accident. The breakthrough was inspired by a bacterium (discovered in 2016 at a waste dump in Japan) that had somehow evolved to eat plastic. Scientists and environmentalists alike hope that the discovery can tackle the vast quantity of bottles, bags and products dumped into landfill and oceans.

BIOLOGISTS

Biologists study the science of life by looking at animals and organisms, their cells and how they function.

Biologists analyse living organisms and try to understand how they exist in their different environments. For example, when looking at humans, biologists explore how the body works, how its functions are affected by external influences and why the body doesn't work properly when affected by illness and disease.

ARISTOTLE

Ancient Greek polymath, Aristotle, is best known as a philosopher, but he was also a biologist, botanist and zoologist. He created one of the first works aimed at classifying living things into groups.

Today, we tend to use genera and species to categorise plants and animals: humans, for instance, belong to the genus *Homo* and the species *sapiens*, forming *Homo sapiens*, in the same way that *T. rex* belongs to the *Tyrannosaurus* genus and the *rex* species. Aristotle's findings were revolutionary at the time; in fact his system was still used until around 200 years ago!

UNDER THE MICROSCOPE

Antonie van Leeuwenhoek was a Dutch scientist during the 17th and 18th centuries. He created powerful lenses, capable of magnifying objects to great effect, and paved the way for microscopes to be used in biology. In fact, Leeuwenhoek crafted more than 500 microscopes during his lifetime.

When observing water through a lens in 1676, Leeuwenhoek inadvertently discovered bacteria. His finding was so spectacular that the famous scientific institution, the Royal Society, elected him a member in 1680.

Robert Hooke is perhaps best known for his work in the realms of physics and architecture, but his discovery of the 'cell' places him firmly in the biology hall of fame.

Hooke, like Leeuwenhoek, was a dab hand at creating and tinkering with microscopes, and, when peering closely at a slice of cork, noticed that the plant matter looked as though it were made from empty vessels, or 'cells'. He also lent his name to Hooke's law – the law of elasticity.

CLONING

When Keith Campbell and Ian Wilmut created Dolly the Sheep in 1996, the pair made history – they had successfully cloned (duplicated) a mammal for the first time from an adult cell. Dolly was generated using a single sheep cell, combined with a process called Somatic Cell Nuclear Transfer, or SCNT for short. The cell then began to divide in order to create an embryo (and eventually a baby). Today, cloning continues, and at the end of 2017, two long-tailed macaques called Zhong Zhong and Hua Hua were created in China using the same technique.

MATHEMATICIANS

Mathematicians can be employed by all sorts of industries. They use numbers, signs and symbols to solve problems.

Some mathematicians become excellent accountants due to their superb numeracy skills; others are employed as economists, to look at trends and to use equations to try and make money; some work as engineers; and others are employed by tech or software companies to create code.

An equation is a mathematical statement that says the two sides of an expression are equal. Take the world's most famous equation, for instance:

$$E = mc^2$$

E stands for Energy
M stands for Mass
C is the Speed of Light

Albert Einstein published this equation in 1905. It explains how stars, like the Sun, convert energy from their gases.

SRINIVASA RAMANUJAN

Srinivasa Ramanujan was born in India in 1887. Despite receiving very little in the way of formal training, Ramanujan had an understanding of mathematics that other contemporaries of his time didn't possess. In other words, he was a genius! When he died in 1920, he left behind three notebooks and a sheaf of papers full of equations and their solutions. Mathematicians studied the pages long after his death, realising that he'd solved all sorts of things that hadn't been published during his lifetime.

$$a^2 + b^2 = c^2$$

COMPUTER PROGRAMMING

Ada Lovelace is regarded as one of the world's first computer programmers. She collaborated with an inventor called Charles Babbage during the 19th century, helping him create some of his contraptions and precursors to the modern-day computer. Ada's research helped pave the way for other programmers and, in the 1980s, a programming language was named after her. 'Ada' was even used by the US Department of Defence.

MARYAM MIRZAKHANI

Maryam Mirzakhani won maths awards when she was still at secondary school, scoring full marks in an International Olympiad in 1995 at the age of 18. In 2014, she became the first woman to win a Fields Medal – the world's most prestigious mathematics award. Before her untimely death in 2017, Maryam taught at some of the best universities in the world, including Harvard, Princeton and Stanford in the USA, inspiring the bright minds of the future.

ARCHIMEDES

Archimedes is one of the most famous mathematicians to have graced the planet. Born in ancient Greece, he spent the majority of his life working on the island of Sicily (now part of Italy), where he helped a king named Hieron II. He used his expertise to create inventions, including the Archimedes screw – a device for dredging, dragging and twisting water up through the ground. He's also famed for his 'Heurēka/Eureka' moment (meaning 'I've found it') when he realised how to calculate whether Hieron II's crown was pure gold by submerging it to determine its volume.

Archimedes is rumoured to have created all sorts of contraptions, including a huge lens capable of concentrating light to burn enemy ships, a working model of the Solar System and a colossal catapult!

DOCTORS & NURSES

Doctors, nurses and medical professionals examine, diagnose and treat patients. They help save lives every single day!

Doctors and nurses can help prevent disease, cure sickness and provide aid to patients on their road to recovery. They have to work well under pressure in an extremely fast-paced working environment.

The standard training to become a doctor can take the best part of a decade, and to become a specialist in a particular field can take a further ten years on top.

Squeamish people need not apply – your average doctor is likely to encounter cuts, scrapes, snot, blood and other bodily fluids on a daily basis!

DID YOU KNOW?
Florence's birthday on May 12th is now celebrated globally as International Nurses Day.

FLORENCE NIGHTINGALE

Florence Nightingale, also known as the 'Lady with the Lamp', is widely regarded as the founder of modern nursing.

During the Crimean War (1853 – 1856) many soldiers were dying from wounds and diseases. Florence realised that cleanliness in hospitals was paramount in preventing the spread of infections, so she helped manage and train nurses, paying strict attention to the state of equipment, hospital food, dressings, blankets and bedding.

Florence worked tirelessly and, as electricity didn't exist at this time, carried a candle-lit lamp so that she could see in the darkness.

After the war, Florence returned home a hero. Queen Victoria even sent her a letter of thanks. In 1860, she set up a medical school in London to help train more nurses. Florence lived to the age of 90 and, during her lifetime, she helped reform the state of hospitals in Britain. Her legacy lives on today!

EDWARD JENNER MAKES HISTORY

Edward Jenner (1749 - 1823)

Edward Jenner was an English doctor and scientist. He is widely credited as being the creator of the world's first vaccine (a form of medicine injected into people to protect them from a disease) to combat a deadly virus called smallpox.

Edward was a keen-eyed observer of the medical world. He saw that dairymaids seemed to be immune to smallpox and started to wonder why. He noticed that most of the maids had been infected with a virus called cowpox at some point in the past and knew there had to be a link.

Edward now had to experiment! He found a girl with cowpox to help him, and took some pus from one of the sores on her body (we told you this wasn't for the faint-hearted!). He then used this pus, placing it within a small cut on the body of a young boy who quickly contracted cowpox.

All was going to plan. When the boy had recovered from cowpox, Edward injected him with smallpox! The virus had no effect, prompting the doctor to inject the poor boy a few more times! The boy still showed no symptoms and Edward's research was published to much acclaim.

In 1980, more than 180 years after Jenner's breakthrough, the world was finally declared free of smallpox. Vaccinations are now used regularly around the world for diseases like polio, measles and mumps, but, unfortunately, not all children have access to these medicines and the diseases still exist in some parts of the world.

TU YOUYOU

In 2015, Tu Youyou received the Nobel Prize for developing artemisinin – a drug used to combat a disease called malaria, which kills hundreds of thousands of people per year. Tu and her team studied more than 2,000 ancient folk remedies to find the right substance. Her breakthrough came when she used cold water, rather than hot water, on the sweet wormwood plant, which led to the creation of artemisinin.

The drug that Tu helped create has been used to treat hundreds of millions of patients.

DID YOU KNOW?
Malaria is transmitted by female Anopheles mosquitoes.

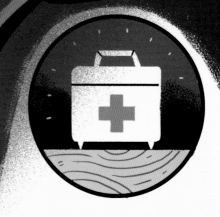

JOSEPH MURRAY
In 1954, Joseph Murray performed the first successful organ transplant by transferring a kidney from one identical twin to the other. Murray's pioneering work has helped save countless lives and organ transplants have become a vital part of modern surgery. Murray received the Nobel Prize in Medicine in 1990.

HAROLD MOODY

Harold Moody was born in Jamaica in 1882. He moved to Britain as a young man, where he trained as a doctor. But, on qualifying, he found it difficult to find work because of the social and racial attitudes of the time. Many hospitals refused to employ black doctors because white patients didn't want to be treated by them.

Undeterred, Harold set up his own doctor's surgery in 1913 to serve the community. His kindness, bravery and dedication transcended the medical field and he became an activist and spokesperson, forming the League of Coloured Peoples in 1931.

SOCIAL WORKERS

Social workers look after the people within a community, especially those more vulnerable than others, by offering support and guidance.

Some aspects of social work are similar to those found in nursing and psychology as social workers pay close attention to the health and wellbeing of the people they visit, especially children or the infirm.

Social workers are sometimes required to make tough decisions, such as whether or not family members should live together, and how often they should spend time with one another.

BARBARA MIKULSKI

Barbara Mikulski studied to become a social worker at university and her work with the impoverished and elderly meant she saw, first-hand, how important it is for human beings to look out for one another.

In the late '60s and early '70s, Barbara began working with the civil rights movement in an attempt to end segregation, whilst continuing her work with the elderly in the American city of Baltimore. In 1986, Mikulski became the first female Democrat to win a seat in both the US Senate and House of Representatives. When she left office in 2017, Mikulski was the longest-serving female member of Congress.

SUDHA MURTY

Born in southwest India in 1950, Sudha Murty was a skilled engineer and computer whizz before she turned her hand to social work.

Sudha used her knowledge and kindness to teach and educate people from all walks of life, provide better health facilities for men and women and help pave the way for the construction of thousands of libraries in India. She used to walk 2km (1.25mi) just to use a toilet at work and campaigned for more toilets to be built in her country. She founded orphanages and fundraised for school computers. As if her list of achievements wasn't quite long enough, she's also an award-winning novelist.

VETS

From arachnids and farm animals, to boa constrictors and bats, vets (short for 'veterinarians') help all sorts of creatures, especially pets, recover from sickness and injury.

Now that you know how long it takes to become a doctor, imagine having to apply that knowledge across different species! It's not just cats and dogs that vets have to treat – livestock, exotic animals and even wild beasts may be on the agenda!

Vets also need to be able to operate under pressure (and with a steady hand) and to make difficult decisions for the wellbeing of each and every animal they see.

DID YOU KNOW?
Just like doctors, some vets must have a 'speciality', meaning they are particularly well-qualified in one specific aspect of the science, or in a specific animal.

You could be a bird boffin, for example.

Or enraptured by reptiles!

DID YOU KNOW?
Many animals, especially mammals, can suffer from the same sicknesses and diseases as humans!

BUSTER LLOYD-JONES

Buster Lloyd-Jones was a British veterinary practitioner. During World War II, he looked after sick, injured and abandoned animals. As people moved away from the danger of the conflict, or as soldiers failed to return home, more and more pets became homeless . . .

Buster, however, helped many of the strays and he ended up housing all sorts of animals, including cats, dogs, monkeys, birds, goats and even snakes.

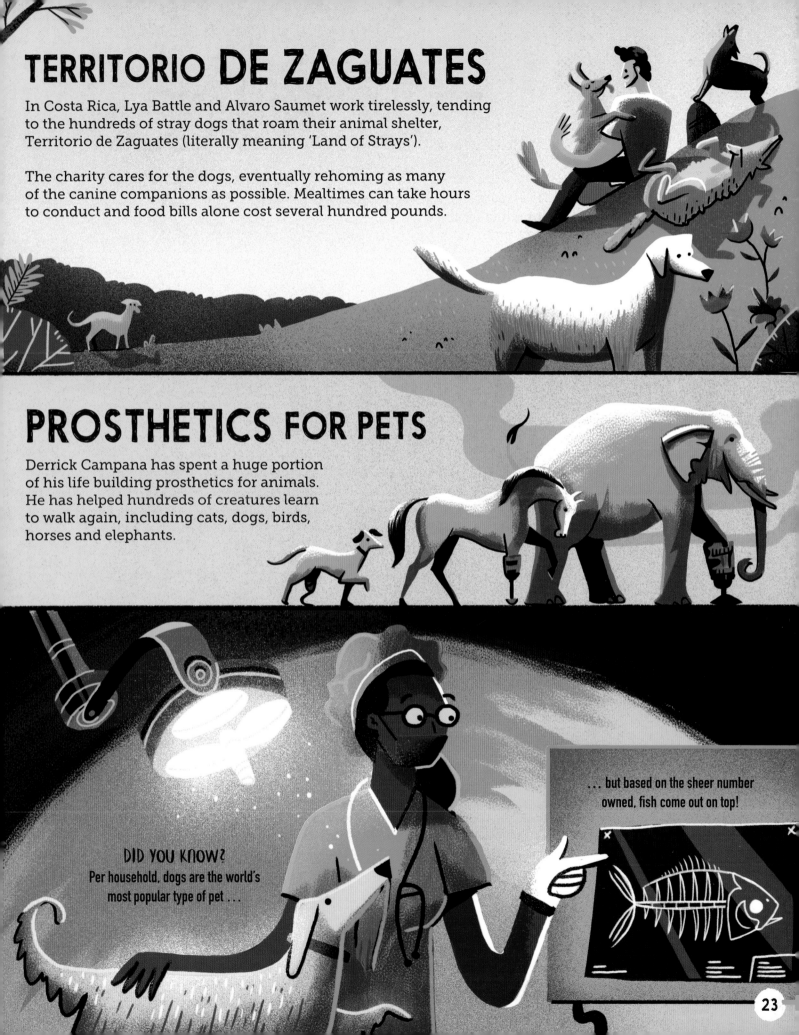

TERRITORIO DE ZAGUATES

In Costa Rica, Lya Battle and Alvaro Saumet work tirelessly, tending to the hundreds of stray dogs that roam their animal shelter, Territorio de Zaguates (literally meaning 'Land of Strays').

The charity cares for the dogs, eventually rehoming as many of the canine companions as possible. Mealtimes can take hours to conduct and food bills alone cost several hundred pounds.

PROSTHETICS FOR PETS

Derrick Campana has spent a huge portion of his life building prosthetics for animals. He has helped hundreds of creatures learn to walk again, including cats, dogs, birds, horses and elephants.

DID YOU KNOW?
Per household, dogs are the world's most popular type of pet . . .

. . . but based on the sheer number owned, fish come out on top!

ATHLETES

Athletes tend to possess extraordinary strength, speed, stamina, agility and skill, not to mention unrivalled determination, passion, dedication and natural talent!

Here are a few of the record breakers, some of whom you may never have heard of, and others who are household names.

USAIN BOLT

The most successful sprinter of all time, Usain Bolt wowed the world when he raced into the history books in 2008, smashing the 100m and 200m records. He won nine Olympic gold medals during his career, breaking his own sprinting records in the process.

LINDSEY VONN

Lindsey Vonn is the world's most successful downhill skier. Her career was plagued by injury, but she overcame adversity time and time again to take her place at the top of the podium.

TRISCHA ZORN

Trischa Zorn is the most decorated athlete in Paralympic Games history, having won 55 medals. She swam in seven separate Games, in a career spanning more than 25 years.

MICHAEL PHELPS

Michael Phelps won more Olympic medals than any other competitor — 23 gold, 3 silver and 2 bronze! This astonishing haul doesn't even take into account all of the other medals he won at additional events and competitions.

STRENGTH

MARIUSZ PUDZIANOWSKI

Mariusz Pudzianowski won the World's Strongest Man title five times.

HAKUHŌ SHŌ

Hakuhō Shō won 13 sumo tournament championships in a row.

ŻYDRŪNAS SAVICKAS

Żydrūnas Savickas won every type of professional strongman competition at least once!

DID YOU KNOW?

British strongman Eddie Hall was the first person to 'deadlift' 500 kg (1,100 lb).

SERENA WILLIAMS

Serena Williams shot to tennis success with her powerful ground strokes and killer serve. In Grand Slam tournaments Serena has won more than 20 singles titles and more than a dozen doubles titles with her sister, Venus.

MICHAEL SCHUMACHER

Michael Schumacher won more Formula 1 Championships and Grand Prix than any other racer. He had an insatiable desire to win and was nicknamed 'The Red Baron' because of the success he achieved with his iconic red Ferrari.

AGILITY

SIMONE BILES

Simone Biles won 19 Olympic and World Championship medals before she was even 20 years old. She is well-known for a move now known as the 'Biles', involving a double backflip with a 180 degree twist added in for extra difficulty!

STEFKA KOSTADINOVA

Stefka Kostadinova has held the women's world record in high jump since 1987!

MICHAEL JORDAN

At 6ft 6in tall, basketball player Michael Jordan was superb at slam-dunking and a master of the 'fadeaway' — a shot performed while jumping away from the target goal in order to dodge defenders.

STAMINA

RAGNHILD MYKLEBUST

Ragnhild Myklebust holds the record for most medals won during the Winter Paralympic Games: 27 in total (22 gold, 3 silver, 2 bronze). Most of her medals were won in cross-country skiing events.

HAILE GEBRSELASSIE

Haile Gebrselassie used to run more than 10 miles (16km) to get to school and back. As a professional long-distance runner he broke multiple world records.

DEAN KARNAZES

Dean Karnazes was capable of running extreme distances in rapid times. He set many records during his career, including running 560km (348mi) in 80 hours and 44 minutes without sleep in 2005!

SKILL

PELÉ

Edson Arantes do Nascimento, known as Pelé, is considered to be the world's greatest footballer. He played in more than 1,300 professional matches and is the only player to win three World Cups. Pelé was also the leading goal scorer for his national team (Brazil) and the most successful league goal scorer in history for his club, Santos.

ROGER FEDERER

Roger Federer has won more Grand Slam (Wimbledon, Australian Open, US Open and French Open) titles than any other player. He's widely regarded as the greatest tennis player the world has ever seen.

He held the No 1 spot in the ATP (Association of Tennis Professionals) ranking system for an astonishing 237 consecutive weeks — and more than 300 weeks in total.

ALL-ROUND

MUHAMMAD ALI

Muhammad Ali is quite possibly the best boxer of all time. After turning professional, he fought 61 bouts, winning 56 of them with his superb stamina, strength and agility. His fame transcended the sporting world and he became a household name, known for his witty mottos and maxims.

REINHILD MÖLLER

At the age of three, Reinhild Möller lost half of her left leg in a farming accident. Since then, Möller has made a name for herself in both the Summer and Winter Paralympic Games, winning 19 gold medals in alpine skiing as well as medals in athletic track-and-field events.

'Float like a butterfly, sting like a bee.'

EXTREME ATHLETES

If ordinary sports seem a little tame, and you'd like a bit more adrenaline in your life, then maybe extreme sports are for you! There are so many to choose from, and some are more hair-raising than others. Here's a selection of the biggest achievements in the world of extreme sports. Could you go one better?

FELIX BAUMGARTNER

In 2012, Felix Baumgartner became the first person to break the speed barrier without being powered by a vehicle. He travelled high into Earth's atmosphere and jumped out of his craft, hurtling towards the planet at a staggering 843.6mph (1357.6kph) before releasing his parachute.

SHAUN WHITE

Before becoming a professional snowboarder, Shaun White tried his hand at skateboarding. He was a natural and it wasn't long before he became a big name in the sport.

It's on slick snow and ice, however, rather than wooden ramps and tarmac, that White truly excels. He's won more freestyle snowboarding trophies than you could shake a stick at, including three Olympic gold medals.

COULD YOU JOIN THE CLUB?

The 'Eight-Thousanders' are the 14 highest peaks on Earth. The mountains are more than 8,000m (26,247ft) high and can all be found in the Himalayan or Karakoram mountain ranges in Asia.

To climb them collectively is perceived to be the greatest achievement in mountaineering. Only a handful of intrepid climbers have actually managed this feat. The first person to do so was Reinhold Messner from Italy. It took him just over 16 years to climb the lot.

In 2018, Rodrigo Koxa rode an 80-foot-tall wave at Nazaré beach in Portugal.

Kealoha Kennelly became a professional surfer at the tender age of 17.

Kelly Slater is the most successful surfing champion in the history of the sport.

Not all extreme sports rely on wind, sea and water. Some can be done on dry land, including skateboarding, BMX, climbing, parkour and many more.

TOM SCHAAR

In 2012, 12-year-old skateboarder Tom Schaar completed the very first 1080-degree spin, shattering legendary skater Tony Hawk's long-standing 900-degree record.

DIVE DOWN DEEP

In 2012, Austrian freediver Herbert Nitsch plunged to a mind-boggling depth of 253m (831ft). He became known as 'The Deepest Man on Earth' after achieving this incredible stunt.

ARMED FORCES

The armed forces help protect countries from violence, threat and invasion. Their services are also often called upon to help when natural disasters, famine, disease or wars affect countries across the globe, even in foreign lands.

Most armed forces are split into land, air and sea services, usually army, air force and navy, respectively.

Each service requires certain skills: fast-jet and helicopter pilots, for instance, need excellent vision and quick reflexes, while specialists in the navy must be strong swimmers. Training can be tough, and extremely physical. Many recruits drop out during the physical tests.

FRANZ STIGLER

During World War II, German pilot Franz Stigler had an opportunity to destroy an enemy B-17 bomber. Instead, he escorted the damaged plane to the English Channel and saluted the American pilot, Charles Brown. 40 years later, Franz and Charles reunited and formed a lasting friendship.

RAYE MONTAGUE

Raye Montague joined the United States Navy in 1956. During her career, she helped revolutionise the process of designing ships and submarines by using computers.

Raye was the first person to design a ship using a computer and the first female to hold such a senior position in her naval department. She helped design all sorts of ships during her career, including the colossal Nimitz-class aircraft carrier.

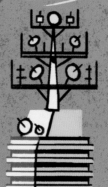

DID YOU KNOW?

A Nimitz-class aircraft carrier can carry more than 80 planes. Because these ships primarily run on nuclear power, they can travel non-stop without the need to refuel.

NADEZHDA POPOVA

Nadezhda Popova played a part in more than 850 missions during World War II. She enlisted in the 588th Night Bomber Regiment when she was just 19 years old and flew as many as 18 times per night. By the time Nadezhda returned to base, her plane was often flecked with bullet holes. Her aircraft was shot down in 1942, but she was uninjured, and while on the ground she met another downed pilot who would later become her husband!

OPERATION RAHAT

Operation Rahat was an enormous rescue operation carried out by the Indian Air Force. In 2013, heavy rains had affected an area in India called Uttarakhand, and helicopters were flown to flooded landscapes in order to provide emergency supplies (including food and medical equipment) and airlift people to safety. During the early stages of the mission, more than 20,000 people were rescued.

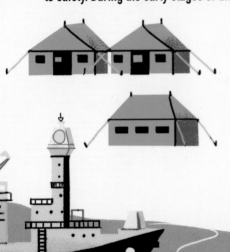

THE GURKHAS

Native to the country of Nepal, the Gurkhas are considered to be amongst the most fierce, fearsome, skilled and brave warriors in the world. Stories of their heroics and gallantry have spanned the globe and many Nepalese soldiers have been awarded medals, including the Victoria Cross (the highest award given by the British Army).

Gurkhas often carry a special curved knife called a *khukuri.*

DID YOU KNOW?
In July 2018, a brave band of Thai Navy SEALs and divers from around the world rescued 12 boys trapped in a submerged cave in northern Thailand. The men had to swim for more than 6 hours to save each boy and the rescue mission took 17 days to orchestrate.

THE INVICTUS GAMES
The Invictus Games is an international sports event, in which injured or sick veterans from countries around the world compete against each other in different sports. The word *invictus* means 'unconquered' in Latin, and its definition pays tribute to the bravery and unwavering determination of the competing athletes.

NEW YORK

The firefighters of New York City are some of the most revered in the world. Each fire company in the city serves a particular district or area and helps the community within it.

When the Twin Towers were engulfed in flames in 2001, the New York City Fire Department deployed hundreds of members of staff to the scene. Fire departments from further afield even travelled to the city to help!

In an act of outstanding heroism and courage, the firefighters worked tirelessly, evacuating thousands of trapped office workers until the towers collapsed. Despite the chaos, emergency workers and New York citizens united, searching through the debris to locate survivors.

Nearly 3,000 people died in the catastrophe, including more than 300 firefighters. A memorial centre now stands where the towers once stood, honouring the lives and memories of those that perished.

FIREFIGHTERS

Firefighters help save lives, protect buildings and rescue wildlife and domestic animals. Fighting fires is one of the most dangerous jobs on the planet.

Would-be firefighters must train for hours on end and be capable of carrying incredibly heavy kit. Gear can weigh up to 35 kg (75 lb) – that's as much as a large dog!

There are plenty of written and practical exams to pass, as well as red-hot temperatures to deal with. The average flame burns at more than 400°C (752°F) and fires can reach temperatures in excess of 1,100°C (2,012°F)!

Perhaps more important than brains and brawn is bravery. To enter a burning building is no mean feat, especially when most other people are trying to run out!

DID YOU KNOW?
A coal mine, located beneath the town of Centralia (Pennsylvania, USA), caught fire in 1962. It is still burning to this very day. Almost all of the town's inhabitants have now fled, but some still remain.

FOREST FIRES IN AUSTRALIA

When temperatures in Australia soar and the landscape becomes very dry, areas of forest can ignite, causing wildfires to spread rapidly across vast areas. These fires can span millions of acres, threatening animals, plants and humans.

Brave firefighters, many of whom are volunteers, help extinguish these enormous infernos. In severe cases, whole towns can be cut off by the blazes, so patrols use radios and weather reports to make sure they don't get caught off guard.

In some instances, aeroplanes brimming with water are flown over afflicted areas. Each plane is capable of dumping in excess of 15,000 litres (3,300 gallons) on to the flames below – that's enough water to fill more than 85 bath tubs!

POLICE

Police help detect and prevent crime.
Just like firefighters, they serve particular districts
and look after the people and property within their borough.

The police force is made up of several divisions and different skills are required for each role. From traffic departments, dog handlers and detectives to underwater search units and undercover intelligence, there are dozens of different roles to choose from! Would you like a canine companion to help you solve crime, would you prefer to travel at high speed in car chases or perhaps you consider yourself more like Sherlock Holmes— the ultimate detective?

Most police forces around the world require cadets to pass written exams, physical tests and basic training, before upping the ante for the more specialised or extreme roles.

FASCINATING FINGERPRINTS

In the 19th century, pioneers of forensic science realised that human fingerprints held the key to solving crime.

In 1881, in order to deter criminals from re-offending, French police officer Alphonse Bertillon started creating an identification system focussing on the measurement of human body parts. By 1883, he'd measured thousands of limbs and identified more than 40 villains in the process. He also began recording fingerprints and photographing faces (later known as 'mugshots').

Subsequently, Juan Vucetich (an Argentine chief police officer) also started to catalogue and record fingerprints. And in 1892, after studying research conducted by a British man called Sir Francis Galton, Vucetich set up the world's first fingerprint bureau.

Vucetich's research was soon put into practice when police were called to a crime at a house owned by Francisca Rojas. After initially suspecting her neighbour, police found a thumbprint at the scene of the crime and compared it with Francisca's ... It was found to be identical. She soon confessed and the case was solved!

Now, more than 100 years later, fingerprints are still catalogued in order to help solve crimes.

DID YOU KNOW?

Japanese police officers sometimes fire paintballs at vehicles involved in crimes. The paint is difficult to wash off, meaning officers still have a shot at finding the culprits even days after the crime has been committed!

A MOST CURIOUS CASE

Luckily, the police are brilliant at cutting crime and excellent at cracking cases. However, not all investigations can be solved! Have a look at these mystifying examples from history.

THE TERMITE GANG

In March 2010, a band of bold burglars burrowed into a bank through neighbouring tunnels. The gang, known as the 'Termites', stole more than £22 million worth of cash and valuables. The bank was closed for renovation, so the burglars spent several days breaking in and many hours clearing out safety deposit boxes.

Before they fled, the Termites lit a fire that set off a sprinkler system, flooding the building. The gang was believed to be linked to a spate of similar crimes that plagued the city of Paris, but no man, or insect, has ever been charged!

AN ART ATTACK

The Isabella Stewart Gardner Museum in Boston, USA, fell victim to one of the world's biggest art heists in 1990. Two men, posing as policemen, stole 13 paintings worth approximately £370 million. Neither the artworks nor the criminals were ever found.

DIAMOND DISASTER

In February, 2013, several men cut through a security fence at Brussels Airport in Belgium, drove towards a stationary plane, and stole £31 million worth of diamonds from on board! Unbelievably, this diamond heist was conducted in broad daylight and plain sight. More than 30 people were arrested during the investigation, but the culprits have never been brought to justice.

DID YOU KNOW?
There's a teddy bear in every Dutch police car!

LAWYERS & JUDGES

Lawyers and judges uphold the laws belonging to their specific country or state, making sure that justice is served and people are given the rights they deserve.

Lawyers and barristers help fight for their client's interests by defending or prosecuting in a court of law, or compiling evidence on their behalf.

Judges, as the title suggests, pass judgement on courtroom proceedings and sentence the guilty. A judge must remain impartial and be proficient in their knowledge of the laws that help govern the land.

DID YOU KNOW?
After being wrongly convicted of a crime in 1992, Derrick Hamilton studied law while locked behind bars. He learned how to prove his innocence and was freed in 2015.

FATOU BENSOUDA

As a child, Fatou Bensouda used to sneak into courtrooms to catch a glimpse of court proceedings. She took a keen interest in the law, and the notion of 'right' and 'wrong', from an early age.

Fatou is now a criminal law prosecutor for the International Criminal Court. It's her job to try and prosecute people who have committed atrocious crimes around the world, especially tyrannical leaders or those involved in war crimes. To date, Fatou has ensured that several villains are, and will remain, behind bars.

VRINDA GROVER

Vrinda Grover is a human rights lawyer in India. Much of her work focusses on women's rights, especially when women are subject to violence.

Vrinda has appeared in many high-profile cases and fought for many clients over the years. She also campaigns for laws (such as the death penalty law in India) to be changed. Thanks to her tenacity, Vrinda is now a spokesperson and advocate for justice, not just in India, but around the world.

DID YOU KNOW?

In 2016, Joshua Browder, a student and computer programmer created a 'lawyer bot' to help homeless people in the UK. The app offers free guidance about government housing and a downloadable application letter, which can be given to a court of law.

The aim of the app was to help the most impoverished and vulnerable people in society find a means of shelter.

BAR PRO BONO UNIT

The Bar Pro Bono Unit is a UK-based charity that provides free legal assistance to people who can't afford it. Every year, the charity acknowledges and awards someone who has offered free legal services to those most in need. In 2017, immigration barrister Tanya Murshed received the award for the incredible work she conducted.

Tanya Murshed trained law students in Uganda, teaching them how to gather and collate evidence for inmates sentenced to death. She also organised training sessions with judges and lawyers.

Thanks to this work, more than two hundred death-row inmates have been resentenced and no longer face the death penalty. In some cases, prisoners were actually released! There's still more to be done, however, and Tanya's tireless work continues ...

ARTISTS

Throughout history, art has allowed people to convey their emotion, imagination, passion and skill without language's limitations. Art has inspired and influenced a whole host of things, including music, fashion and design.

Art is not just about drawing, painting and sculpture – it encompasses all sorts of things, from film to music and dance. Most artists start their careers by going to art college, university or specialist classes. Some artists, however, are entirely self taught.

To create art requires skill and style. The most successful artists have a signature approach or technique that sets their work apart from the rest of the competition.

LEONARDO DA VINCI

Leonardo Da Vinci's list of talents was so long, and his knowledge so broad, that he could feature on almost any page in this book. But he's perhaps best known for being one of the most accomplished painters in history.

His famous canvas, *Mona Lisa*, now in the Louvre gallery in Paris, France, is one of the most-viewed and visited artworks in the world – more than seven million people flock to see it every year!

DID YOU KNOW?
Surrealist artist Salvador Dali designed the Chupa Chups logo.

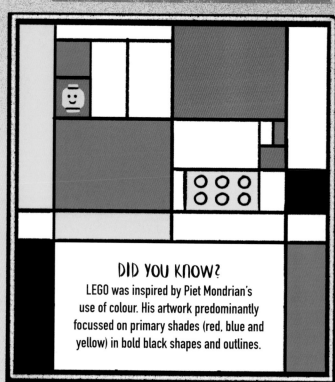

DID YOU KNOW?
LEGO was inspired by Piet Mondrian's use of colour. His artwork predominantly focussed on primary shades (red, blue and yellow) in bold black shapes and outlines.

VINCENT VAN GOGH

Vincent Van Gogh was one of the forefathers of a style of art known as Post-Impressionism. He created more than 850 paintings, including *The Starry Night* and *Sunflowers*. Though Van Gogh received little acclaim during his short life, he is now seen as one of the most talented painters in history. In 1990, his painting, *Portrait of Dr Gachet*, sold for £150 million.

Van Gogh fought a constant battle with mental illness. He gained notoriety for cutting off part of his ear and created a few self-portraits depicting his bandaged head. Some critics believe that his best works were created during bouts of depression, and that the colours he used were dependent on mood.

Vincent Van Gogh (1853 - 1890)

FRIDA KAHLO

Frida Kahlo was born with polio, and suffered from injuries and illnesses throughout her life. Despite this, she found solace in her art. Known for her candid self-portraits and colourful depictions of wildlife and nature, Kahlo completed more than 140 paintings.

Though, like Van Gogh, she didn't achieve much recognition during her lifetime, Kahlo is now considered one of the greats and her paintings fetch millions of pounds at auction.

Frida Kahlo (1907 - 1954)

BANKSY

Banksy is not only an artist, he's also an activist. His politically-charged murals, sculptures and stencils often mock or comment on social issues such as surveillance, poverty and penal corruption. His identity remains unknown to all but a few of his closest confidantes.

DID YOU KNOW?
In November, 2017, one of Da Vinci's 500-year-old paintings, *Salvator Mundi*, sold for a record-breaking sum of $450,312,500!

MUSICIANS & COMPOSERS

Musicians and composers convey emotions and stories through musical notes, lyrics, sounds and sheet music.

Music can be beautiful, powerful and evoke certain feelings, it can also be delicate, soft or full of fury! People often consider music a language or form of art.

Some musicians make their millions from album sales and tours, while others perform to just a handful of people or write songs. Likewise, some musicians study to become virtuosos in all sorts of instruments and others play in a band or as a hobby.

There are dozens of musical genres and hundreds of instruments to choose from, or you may even decide you'd rather sing!

DID YOU KNOW?
Musical exams are called 'grades'. Most musicians are assessed from Grade One to Grade Eight, with the latter being the most difficult to obtain.

DID YOU KNOW?
The Beatles licensed their image to many strange products during their illustrious career, including bubble bath and handkerchiefs!

THE BEATLES

The Beatles are the world's most successful band. They've had more Number One albums and singles in the UK and US than any other group, and their records are still sold all over the world. The Beatles transformed the musical charts in the 1960s and created a frenzy wherever they travelled. 'Beatlemania' spread and the band's celebrity status rocketed to unprecedented levels.

MOZART

Wolfgang Amadeus Mozart's musical prowess was evident from an early age. At three years old, he could play chords on his harpsichord and by five he was composing music. Mozart's understanding of his craft was so profound, in fact, that he is rumoured to have been able to play a violin without being shown. He could even memorise music and translate sequences of musical notes from subtle sounds to notes on a page.

Mozart's father, Leopold, was also a musician and helped hone his son's talent by taking him to Italy. It was here that Mozart saw his first opera, which inspired him to write and compose his own at the tender age of 12.

Mozart continued to write music until his death in 1791, by which time he had created more than 40 symphonies, in excess of 20 operas and approximately 600 pieces of music in total. He amassed a loyal fanbase during his lifetime and his works were well-known throughout Europe, where he travelled extensively. Despite his triumphs, he died an exceptionally poor man.

Nevertheless, Mozart's legacy lives on ... his music is still performed around the world and a play based on his life is often staged in theatres and became an Academy Award-winning film.

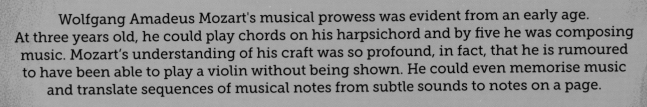

HILDEGARD OF BINGEN

Hildegard of Bingen lived more than 900 years ago and her impact on music during the Middle Ages was profound.

She composed dozens of songs and wrote lyrics to accompany many of them. The only way of popularising music at the time was by performing to audiences or transcribing the musical notes. It is thought that Hildegard may have performed some of her songs to clergymen and women on her travels around European monasteries, possibly forming one of the first musical tours in history!

DID YOU KNOW?
Mozart's party trick involved playing the piano while the keys were covered with a cloth.

ACTIVISTS

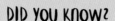

Activists campaign to bring about social, political and economic reform. Though anyone can be an activist, some people are so vehemently passionate about certain causes that they campaign full time.

Activism can take many different forms, from petitions and charitable donations to street marches and protests. The goal of an activist is to make the world a better place.

Activists often fight for causes close to their hearts or those that affect them directly. Many fight to protect the environment, to pursue equal opportunities for men and women of all races and to make sure the most impoverished and vulnerable people in society receive fair treatment.

Many brave people have campaigned for change in the past and will continue to do so long into the future.

DID YOU KNOW?
In July, 2018, a Swedish student stopped a man from being deported (forced to leave a country) after she refused to sit down whilst aboard an aeroplane.

Despite receiving a backlash from several passengers, Elin Ersson stood defiant, making sure the passenger was allowed to exit the plane, rather than forced to return to his war-torn country.

HARRIET TUBMAN
Harriet Tubman was an American abolitionist and political activist. She escaped from slavery when she was 27 years old and helped more than 70 other men, women and children flee from the slave states in America. When a civil war erupted between northern (Union) and southern (Confederate) states, Tubman enlisted as a spy in the Union Army. She later campaigned for women's suffrage (right to vote).

MALALA YOUSAFZAI
Malala Yousafzai was outspoken in her campaign for women's educational rights in Pakistan. When Malala was just 15 years old, she was shot for her beliefs by a Taliban fighter. She recovered from her wounds and continued to crusade for educational rights. Her story was broadcast around the world and, in 2014, she was awarded the Nobel Peace Prize for her activism.

AI WEIWEI

Ai Weiwei's activism is primarily voiced through his art. In 2016 he tied 14,000 life vests around the pillars of the Konzerthaus in Berlin, Germany. The life jackets were all from asylum seekers, forced to flee Syria on their way to the European continent. The installation gained media attention and helped emphasise the plight of the Syrian refugees.

MARTIN LUTHER KING JR

Martin Luther King Jr was a focal figure for the civil rights movement during the 1950s and '60s in America. He campaigned for African Americans to have the same legal rights as others by means of peaceful protests and political gatherings. His 'I Have A Dream' speech, is widely regarded as the most important oration of the 20th century.

ISHMAEL BEAH

Ishmael Beah was forced to fight as a child soldier in a bitter civil war in Sierra Leone for more than three years before he was rescued. Despite returning to normal life, it wasn't long before he had to flee yet more violence as fighting raged across the country.

Ishmael eventually made his way to New York, USA, where he continued his education. He wrote about his tumultuous experiences and memories in a successful book, *A Long Way Gone*.

POLITICIANS

Politicians help govern their countries, counties, cities or towns and look after the interests of the people under their jurisdiction.

Politics affects almost everything, from economics and budgets to laws and education. A politician helps look after the interests of their constituency (area). A Prime Minister, President or political leader will look after their country and the people within it, whereas a Mayor may just have their city or town's best interests at heart.

'Real leaders must be ready to sacrifice all for the freedom of their people.'

NELSON MANDELA

Nelson Mandela began his political career as a lawyer and established South Africa's first black law practice in 1952. He hoped to rid his country of the apartheid laws passed by the South African government in 1948, which denied black people the right to vote.

Mandela's activism saw him regularly detained by authorities, and, in 1964, he was arrested and sentenced to life imprisonment. Mandela was eventually released in 1990, having spent over twenty-six years behind bars. He won the Nobel Peace Prize in 1993 for his efforts to end apartheid.

Mandela became the first president of a democratic South Africa in 1994, and created housing, education and development programmes designed to help black communities.

His aura of morality and kindness was so prevalent that his death, on 5th December 2013, wasn't just mourned by people from South Africa but by men and women from all around the world.

ANEURIN BEVAN

Born into a Welsh working-class mining community in 1897, Aneurin Bevan was elected a Member of Parliament in 1929 and overcame a speech impediment to become one of the best public speakers of the time. In 1948, he founded the National Health Service (NHS) in the UK, which guaranteed free healthcare for all citizens and continues to do so to this day.

Bevan also developed housing programmes to help some of the country's poorest people, building over one million new homes before 1950.

Through his campaigning and policies, Bevan helped save countless lives in a United Kingdom still recovering from the devastating aftermath of World War II.

MAHATMA GANDHI

Mohandas Karamchand Gandhi was an Indian advocator of human rights. As a teenager, he wanted to become a doctor, but eventually trained as a lawyer, travelling to England to begin his studies.

When the British Government pushed through laws which allowed them to imprison people without trial in India, Gandhi responded by leading a series of peaceful political protests against British occupation. In 1930 he organised the Salt March, walking 240 miles towards the sea to collect the precious commodity from its source. The aim was to boycott British salt which incurred an unfair level of tax and which natives were banned from selling. Word of the Salt March spread and many people were galvanised by Gandhi's actions.

By the end of the uprising, some 60,000 people had been imprisoned by police.

Gandhi staged many non-violent protests during his lifetime and his stance as an unyielding pacifist inspired a nation. India eventually gained its independence in 1947, marking the beginning of the end of the British Empire.

ARCHITECTS & BUILDERS

Architects and builders help design and construct the structures we sleep, work, shop, sit, eat and shelter in.

From humble homes and huge hospitals to super-sized stadiums and skyscrapers, the creation of buildings relies on teamwork. Many people with different jobs are required to help a building come to fruition.

Architects use skills in mathematics, drawing and sometimes engineering to plan and design buildings.

Builders use brawn, construction expertise, heavy machinery and communication skills to ensure that projects are completed.

Large-scale builds also require project managers, surveyors and engineers to help with the plans and regulations.

DID YOU KNOW?

The Jeddah Tower in Saudi Arabia is set to be the first building to soar more than 1km (3,280ft) into the sky. Construction began in 2013, but, since then, progress has slowed. If all goes to plan, this staggering skyscraper will claim the title as the world's tallest building, knocking Burj Khalifa (828m/2,717ft) in Dubai from the top spot.

MIMAR SINAN

Born in 1490, Mimar Sinan helped create more than 300 structures, including 79 mosques, 34 palaces and 19 tombs, revolutionising the architectural style in the Ottoman Empire. Some of his most iconic buildings, including the Şehzade Mosque and the Mosque of Süleyman I the Magnificent (both in the city of Istanbul, Turkey) can still be seen today.

DID YOU KNOW?

Despite being the smallest of the three main pyramids at Giza in Egypt, approximately 10,000 workers were required to build The Pyramid of Menkaure.

ANTONI GAUDÍ

Antoni Gaudí's architectural style was inspired by the patterns and shapes he saw in the natural world. He helped design many buildings, but his most famous, Sagrada Família in Barcelona, Spain, remains unfinished. Gaudí spent much of his life as lead architect on the project but, despite this, the cavernous church was less than 25% complete when he died in 1926.

The grand building is now in its final stages of completion, but it has taken more than 130 years to reach this milestone!

'Nothing is art if it does not come from nature.'

FRANK LLOYD WRIGHT

Regarded as the 'godfather' of modern architecture, Frank Lloyd Wright designed more than 1,000 structures before his death in 1959. His most famous building, the Guggenheim Museum in New York, USA, features a spiral ramp flowing through its centre.

DID YOU KNOW?
The Great Mosque of Djenné in Mali, is the largest mud building in the world.

ENGINEERS

Engineers plan and build the infrastructure around us,
designing buildings, products, technology, machines and more.

From building bridges and colossal stadiums, to electricity pylons
and transport systems, engineers have helped shape our surroundings.

There are different types of engineers, including mechanical, structural,
aeronautical, electrical, product and chemical. Engineers have to be able
to understand how things work and how they can be improved. They
tend to possess a wealth of mathematical and scientific knowledge.

To date, engineers have allowed us to travel the world,
soar the skies and land on the Moon. They've also
developed ways of communicating over long
distances and created inventions
that help save lives.

JOSEPH STRAUSS

Joseph Strauss was an American engineer.
In 1902 he founded his own building company,
specialising in bridge construction.

In the early 1920s, San Francisco's city planners wanted to build
a huge bridge to span the one-mile wide bay, connecting their city with
Marin County. On hearing this news, Strauss presented his design for the
Golden Gate Bridge. At almost two miles in length, it was twice as long as
any existing bridge, and planners were reluctant to commission the design
because of how bold and innovative it was. Nevertheless, Strauss won
the project and the rest is history! Today, the Golden Gate Bridge
is one of the most iconic landmarks in the world.

SHERIEN ELAGROUDY

As more companies produce plastic and packaging and more people throw away rubbish and waste, it becomes harder to store or bury refuse in landfill. Luckily, many engineers and scientists are looking at ways in which we can reduce waste and recycle instead.

Sherien Elagroudy is an Environmental Engineering Professor and an expert in waste management. While at university she helped form a campus-wide recycling system with other students. The team collectively saved tonnes of litter from being thrown into landfill. Since then, Sherien has won several awards for her hard work and unerring dedication to her field.

DID YOU KNOW?
Not only did Gustave Eiffel, nicknamed the 'magician of iron', help construct the Eiffel Tower in Paris and a whole host of bridges in France, he also designed the framework for the Statue of Liberty, which was given to the American people by the French in 1886.

ELON MUSK
As an engineer, Elon Musk is particularly keen to promote the ways in which we can produce green energy, and reduce the devastating effect that burning fossil fuels has on the planet.

Musk has designed and built all manner of things and is the co-founder of several global companies, including Tesla, Inc. (a company that produces electric cars, batteries and solar panels) and SpaceX (a business that aims to make space travel accessible to the public).

Musk also co-founded the Tesla Gigafactory — an enormous structure in Nevada, USA, that produces batteries on a grand scale. The factory is still being built, and will be one of the world's largest structures in terms of square footage when complete.

NIKOLA TESLA

Nikola Tesla was an electrical engineer and an incredible inventor, responsible for some of the most vital breakthroughs in electrical science, including his discovery of alternating current (AC).

Before Tesla's development, the exclusive form of electricity was direct current (DC), which could only be transmitted short distances. Thanks to Tesla's discovery, however, power plants no longer had to be built near people's homes, massively reducing the number of those subjected and exposed to noxious fumes on a daily basis!

Tesla went on to invent the Tesla coil, which could fire bolts of lightning and light up bulbs across his lab. The coil design made it possible to wirelessly transmit electricity, including radio signals (which are still used in radios and televisions today).

BOOKER T WASHINGTON

Booker Taliaferro Washington, more commonly known as Booker T Washington, was born into slavery and, after leaving the plantation, moved to West Virginia. Stricken with poverty and craving an education, Booker found work in a salt furnace aged just nine years old. He used the money he made to subsidise his schooling and, after he graduated, taught children by day and adults by night, offering African Americans of all ages the right to an education.

$$ax = b$$
$$\frac{a}{a}x = \frac{b}{a}$$
$$x = \frac{b}{a}$$

TEACHERS

Teachers help their pupils learn about different subjects, educating and supporting them and helping them achieve their goals.

Teachers inspire the bright minds of the future by sharing passion and imparting knowledge. To become a teacher or professor, applicants must pass certain exams, or excel in one area, or areas, of academia. Most lecturers at college or universities, for example, specialise in a particular field and many will have completed doctoral degrees.

Teaching is an incredibly dynamic profession and one that differs from class to class and from day to day. Teachers can educate an array of age groups, instruct different subjects and work with people from all walks of life.

$$\frac{1}{x} = a$$
$$x = \frac{1}{a}$$

LOUIS BRAILLE

Louis Braille developed the Braille system of reading for the blind. He, himself, was blinded in an accident when he was three years old, but excelled at school and grew up to become a history, geometry and algebra teacher.

ARISTOTLE

Aristotle, an ancient Greek philosopher and scientist, tutored future kings, including Alexander the Great, Ptolemy and Cassander. Aristotle, himself, was tutored by Plato — another famous philosopher.

SAYA

In 2004, Professor Hiroshi Kobayashi created a robot teacher named Saya. Saya taught Science and Technology to ten-year-olds in Tokyo, Japan, and was originally programmed to work as a receptionist. The robot was designed to look like a human and is capable of expressing six emotions - anger, disgust, fear, happiness, sadness and surprise. Hiroshi hopes that robots like Saya can be used to combat teacher shortages in schools around the world.

KAKENYA NTAIYA

The traditions of the Maasai tribe in Kenya and Tanzania dictate that women should leave school at an early age to become housewives. Dr Kakenya Ntaiya, however, broke the mould when she went to college in the USA. Before she left, she made a promise to her village that she would return to help educate the community.

In 2008, Kakenya fulfilled her promise when she founded a boarding school called the Kakenya Center for Excellence, offering a free education to the girls who study there.

TORU KUMON

Toru Kumon, a Japanese Maths Professor, invented the Kumon Method after attempting to enhance his son's numeracy skills.

In 1954, Toru created worksheets for his son to solve and soon found signs of dramatic improvement. The tuition really paid off, and the first Maths Centre using Kumon worksheets opened in 1955.

Today, the Kumon Method is available in more than 50 countries and more than 4 million people use it to learn maths.

DID YOU KNOW?
The Varkey Foundation awards the annual Global Teacher Prize for an outstanding contribution to the teaching profession. The prize is sometimes referred to as the Nobel Prize for teaching, and awards $1 million to the victor.

DID YOU KNOW?
Before becoming the First Lady of the USA in 1933, Eleanor Roosevelt taught History and Literature.

AYUB MOHAMUD

Ayub Mohamud teaches Business Studies and Islamic Studies in Kenya. He also teaches his pupils about tolerance, pacifism and how to respect others, no matter what their religion, colour, culture or class. He encourages students to look at the world around them and to combat some of the issues that affect it. His pupils, for example, produced roof tiles from plastic waste in order to help the lives of slum dwellers, whilst also putting plastic to another purpose.

THE KHAN ACADEMY
Salman Amin Khan founded a free online education platform and YouTube channel called The Khan Academy in 2008. Salman's brainwave came when he was tutoring his cousin on the internet, and his lessons and resources are now watched by as many as 15 million people every month.

WRITERS

Writers help communicate and commentate on social issues, and convey emotions, facts and fictions through written media.

Some writers have catalysed social change, sparked revolutions and ignited political beliefs, some have found fame and monetary success and others have been chastised and imprisoned for their works. The written word can be an extremely powerful tool, prompting the creation of the famous adage that 'the pen is mightier than the sword'. Indeed, writing can be used to convey all sorts of information and to reach as big an audience as possible, or as a private means of communication; take a simple letter, email or text message, for instance.

Some writers produce works of fiction, others concentrate on facts by writing reports and articles for magazines and newspapers. Although the industry is competitive, the great thing is that almost anyone can write – all you need is a pen and paper, or a computer and keyboard. Why not give it a go?

DID YOU KNOW?
There are over 130 million published books in existence.

DID YOU KNOW?
One in ten adults around the world cannot read or write.

OCTAVIA BUTLER

Despite her dyslexia, and numerous rejections from publishers, Octavia E Butler never gave up on her dream of becoming an author. She juggled multiple jobs, including dish washing, in order to make ends meet, waking in the middle of the night to practise her writing. Her hard work eventually paid off, and Butler went on to become one of the most successful and groundbreaking sci-fi authors of all time, winning Hugo and Nebula awards for science fiction writing in the process.

WILLIAM
SHAKESPEARE

William Shakespeare is often cited as the most talented wordsmith in history. He wrote 37 plays and 154 sonnets (poems) in his lifetime, and his works are still studied, performed, loved and lauded today.

From tragedies; such as *Hamlet*, *Othello* and *Macbeth*, to comedies; such as *Twelfth Night* and *A Midsummer Night's Dream*, Shakespeare was a master dramatist. He even wrote historical plays about famous kings. The Bard's works have been performed in almost every country in the world and translated into dozens of languages.

Despite his literary legacy, however, historians are still unsure of William Shakespeare's precise birth date and whether more literary works can be accredited to him. His life may be shrouded in mystery, but his legacy lives on.

J K ROWLING

The most successful author of modern times, Rowling rose to fame when the first book of her Harry Potter series was published in Britain in 1997. Her manuscript was notoriously rejected by more than ten publishers, but she persevered.

Today, her writing has helped inspire reluctant readers on a global scale and transformed the fantasy genre, catapulting it firmly into the mainstream. Despite living below the poverty line while writing *The Philosopher's Stone*, Rowling is now one of the wealthiest people in the world, and she donates millions of pounds to charity every year.

DID YOU KNOW?
J K Rowling dropped off a list of the world's wealthiest people because she gave away so much money to charity!

CHARLES DICKENS

Charles Dickens was forced to leave school when he was just 12 years old in order to work in a shoe warehouse. He toiled for ten hours a day polishing boots, and lived an impoverished life until he found success with his writing. Dickens became one of the most famous authors of his time, creating stories that focussed on penniless protagonists facing a reality not too dissimilar from his own childhood conditions.

THE PEN IS MIGHTIER
THAN THE SWORD

Writers don't always create stories and articles. Some draft religious works, scientific journals, political ideologies, pamphlets, poetry and more. Karl Marx and Friedrich Engels, for instance, published *The Communist Manifesto* in 1848. Despite being only 23 pages long, the pamphlet changed the course of history and led to political uprisings and unrest across Europe as the working classes (proletariat) rallied against the middle and upper classes (the bourgeoisie).

DID YOU KNOW?

The Nobel Prize in Literature is one of the most prestigious accolades a writer can win. The prize is awarded annually to an author who is deemed to have made an outstanding contribution to the literary field. Previous winners include Sir Winston Churchill, Ernest Hemingway, Jean-Paul Sartre, John Steinbeck, Pablo Neruda, Nadine Gordimer and Bob Dylan.

INVENTORS

Inventors make contraptions, machines, software and products in order to solve problems or improve efficiency. Some inventors make things for fun, or simply to see what they're capable of!

Humankind has always sought to make life easier. The invention of the wheel in 3500 BCE, for example, allowed humans to transport much heavier loads over greater distances, and large-scale nail making during Roman times meant people could create bigger and better buildings and ships.

This is still the case today, and modern inventions include cures for diseases, improvements in transport speed and safety, efficiency in businesses and much more.

THOMAS EDISON

Thomas Edison held a record-breaking 1,093 patents in his lifetime, the most famous of which was for the light bulb. He played a pivotal role in the way electricity could be applied to products in the late 19th and early 20th centuries.

As a boy, Edison rarely attended school and suffered from acute hearing problems. He left school and began working on railways before studying telegraphy – the science of using and producing communication systems.

By the 1870s, Edison was a fully-fledged inventor and he went on to create incredible contraptions, including the movie camera, phonograph (a means of recording sound) and the world's first industrial research laboratory.

When he died in 1931, Edison's breath was reportedly captured in a test tube now housed in the Henry Ford Museum (Michigan, USA).

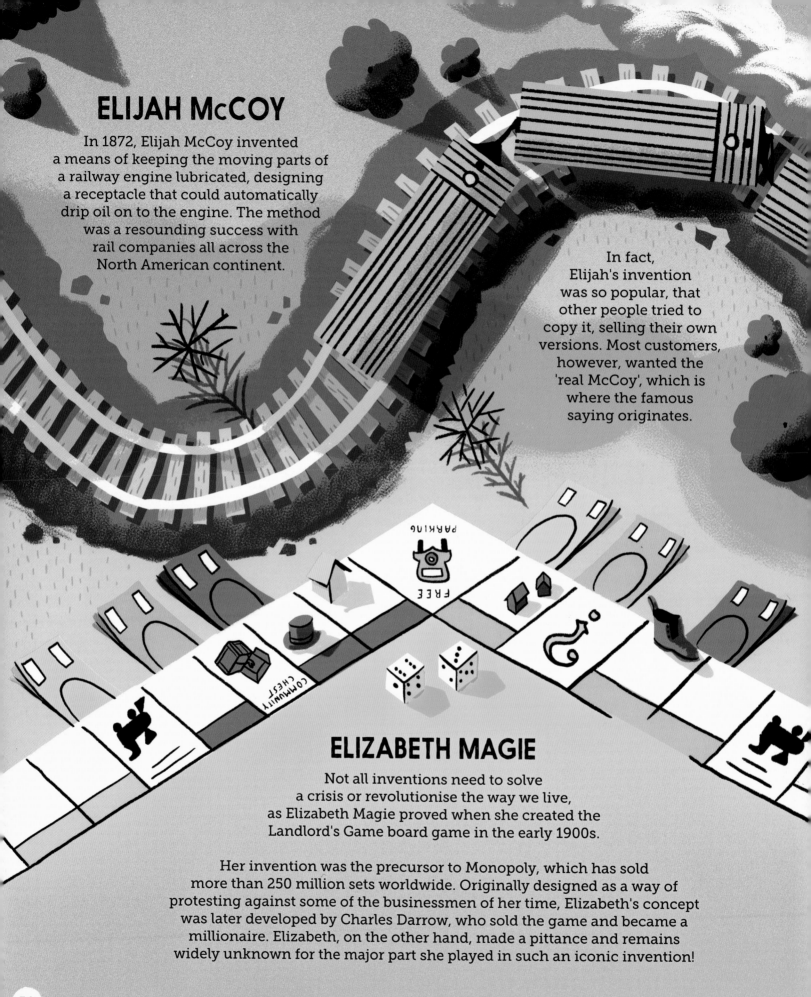

ELIJAH McCOY

In 1872, Elijah McCoy invented a means of keeping the moving parts of a railway engine lubricated, designing a receptacle that could automatically drip oil on to the engine. The method was a resounding success with rail companies all across the North American continent.

In fact, Elijah's invention was so popular, that other people tried to copy it, selling their own versions. Most customers, however, wanted the 'real McCoy', which is where the famous saying originates.

ELIZABETH MAGIE

Not all inventions need to solve a crisis or revolutionise the way we live, as Elizabeth Magie proved when she created the Landlord's Game board game in the early 1900s.

Her invention was the precursor to Monopoly, which has sold more than 250 million sets worldwide. Originally designed as a way of protesting against some of the businessmen of her time, Elizabeth's concept was later developed by Charles Darrow, who sold the game and became a millionaire. Elizabeth, on the other hand, made a pittance and remains widely unknown for the major part she played in such an iconic invention!

3-D PRINTING

Just like the creation of the internet, 3-D printing has been honed and adapted by inventors all around the world. Since its initial conception in the 1980s, 3-D printing has gone from strength to strength, and is now widely used to create a range of products from molten plastic and metal, including models, and parts of cars and machines.

Its applications are becoming more varied (doctors now use the technology to create prosthetics and skin grafts) and it is thought that in the future, 3-D printing machines may be as commonplace as fridge-freezers and washing machines in people's homes.

DID YOU KNOW?

Stephanie Kwolek invented a material called kevlar in 1964. Well known for its incredible strength, kevlar is used to make tennis racquets, frying pans, ropes and bulletproof vests.

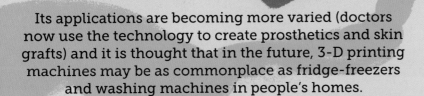

THE FUTURE OF TECH

So what are inventors working on now? Aside from self-driving cars, jet packs, spacecraft and alternative energy sources, Artificial Intelligence is widely considered to be the next big step. Computers have been created with mind-blowing capabilities, and robots are now able to engage in conversation and dialogue. Experts think that AI may become so advanced in the next 50 years that books could be written by robots!

MÁRIA TELKES

Growing concerns related to climate change, ecology, our reliance on plastics and use of fossil fuels have urged many inventors to attempt to alleviate the damage caused by seeking alternative solutions, including biodegradable packaging, wind turbines, electric cars and solar power.

Mária Telkes is credited with creating the first solar-powered heating system for houses and, in 1948, the first solar-heated house. Mária also made a solar distiller – a machine capable of converting salt water into drinking water for thirsty soldiers and captains at sea. Her inventions were groundbreaking and have helped inspire domestic solar technology today, including the solar panels that people use to power their homes.

DID YOU KNOW?
Though papyrus and parchments were used long before the 1st century CE, Cai Lun (62–121 CE), is credited with inventing paper in China almost 2,000 years ago.

DID YOU KNOW?
In 1903, the world-famous Wright Brothers successfully designed, built and flew the first powered aircraft. Nowadays, there are more than 100,000 flights per day.

THE INTERNET

The Internet is used by billions of people worldwide and has revolutionised the way that humans access information, view entertainment and socialise with one another. The internet was developed by many people over a long period of time, most notably Lawrence Roberts (one of the forerunners) and Tim Berners-Lee (the inventor of the World Wide Web), showing just how successful computer scientists can be when they collaborate and develop ideas.

FARMERS

Farmers help feed the world's population by growing crops, rearing livestock and making sure the land is fertile enough to produce food.

It goes without saying that farmers require plenty of land in order to do their jobs. In Australia and the USA, for instance, farms can be as large as some European countries.

Farming hours tend to be long, especially during seasons of harvest or birth, and a farmer's produce is often at the mercy of the weather. Nevertheless, the job is one of the most important in the world.

Farms (and the knowledge required to run them) are often passed from generation to generation within families, and agricultural labour is becoming increasingly sought-after around the world.

Arable farmers produce crops.
Pastoral farmers raise animals.
Mixed farmers do both!

GEORGE CARVER

For crops to grow, it's vital that there are enough nutrients (especially the element nitrogen) in the soil. George Carver's research into this was pivotal in preventing soil from becoming infertile. He urged farmers to grow crops, such as sweet potatoes, soybeans and peanuts, which actively replenish soil nutrients whilst also producing food! George wasn't a farmer himself, but his research helped hundreds of American farmers during the 19th and 20th centuries. He was also particularly passionate about peanuts, and is partly responsible for their popularity today!

SOYBEANS

SWEET POTATO

PEANUTS

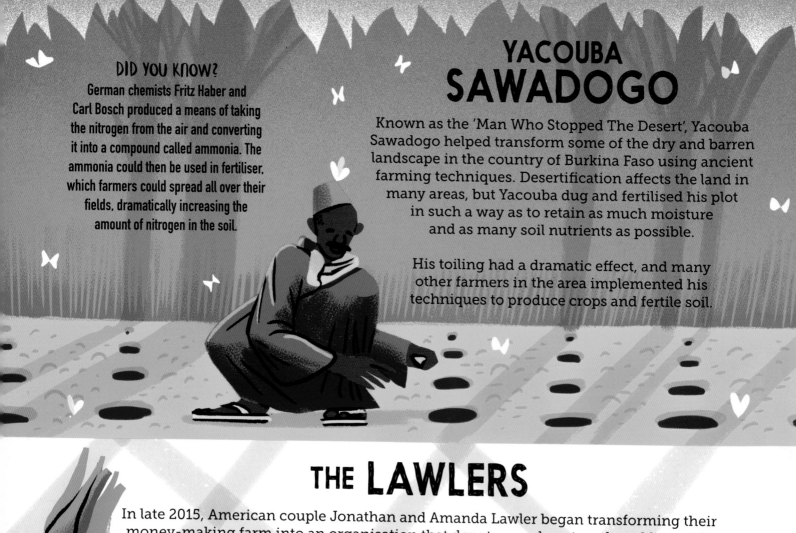

Known as the 'Man Who Stopped The Desert', Yacouba Sawadogo helped transform some of the dry and barren landscape in the country of Burkina Faso using ancient farming techniques. Desertification affects the land in many areas, but Yacouba dug and fertilised his plot in such a way as to retain as much moisture and as many soil nutrients as possible.

His toiling had a dramatic effect, and many other farmers in the area implemented his techniques to produce crops and fertile soil.

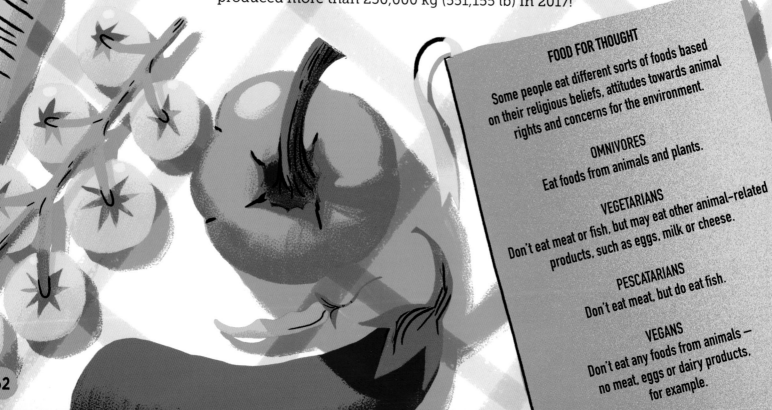

THE LAWLERS

In late 2015, American couple Jonathan and Amanda Lawler began transforming their money-making farm into an organisation that donates produce to vulnerable people in the community. After investing their personal finances, Jonathan and Amanda formed Brandywine Creek Farms. 2016 was the first growing season, which produced more than 190,000 kg (419,000 lb) of food. The farm produced more than 250,000 kg (551,155 lb) in 2017!

FOOD FOR THOUGHT
Some people eat different sorts of foods based on their religious beliefs, attitudes towards animal rights and concerns for the environment.

OMNIVORES
Eat foods from animals and plants.

VEGETARIANS
Don't eat meat or fish, but may eat other animal-related products, such as eggs, milk or cheese.

PESCATARIANS
Don't eat meat, but do eat fish.

VEGANS
Don't eat any foods from animals — no meat, eggs or dairy products, for example.

CONSERVATIONISTS & ENVIRONMENTALISTS

Conservationists and environmentalists collectively help protect the planet's flora, fauna, habitats and ecosystems.

The work that environmentalists (protectors of the environment) and conservationists (protectors of animal species) do is inextricably linked, as one often depends on the other.

Issues such as global warming, plastic consumption, climate change and pollution are all affecting our planet. The good news is that we can all do our bit to keep our world healthy.

WANGARI MAATHAI

In 1977, Wangari Maathai founded the Green Belt Movement, an organisation aimed at combatting deforestation in Kenya. The movement encouraged women to pay closer attention to the environment, and to plant trees in their local areas. The idea was so successful that it spread to neighbouring countries. Thanks to the organisation and its members, more than 51 million trees have been planted to date.

Wangari Maathai won the Nobel Peace Prize in 2004, becoming the first black African woman to receive a Nobel award.

BOYAN SLAT

Boyan Slat, a Dutch inventor, created a means of extracting plastic waste from the ocean, and founded The Ocean Cleanup in 2013.

The organisation is comprised of more than 80 people whose collective goal is to rid the aquatic world of as much plastic as possible.

SOLVING DEFORESTATION

Trees across the world are being cut down at an astonishing rate. Many creatures, including orangutans, gorillas, leopards and tigers may struggle to survive if they lose their habitat. Luckily, however, some people are doing all they can to protect the world's forests and the animals that live in them.

To deter people from cutting down trees in Borneo, Hotlin Ompusunggu created an initiative whereby villagers are rewarded with healthcare discounts if they dissuade loggers from encroaching on their land and felling trees. If villagers plant trees they are also entitled to the same benefits, and more than 120,000 trees have been planted since Hotlin's brilliant plan sprang into action.

Over the years, Indonesia has been severely affected by deforestation. The World Wildlife Foundation (WWF) is doing its best to protect Indonesia's ecosystems by supporting local people and farmers, ensuring that they get good prices for produce and that their methods are sustainable.

Honey production in the country, for instance, has changed dramatically, and farmers are now making sure hives are left intact once honey has been collected. In this way, the hive can be rebuilt and the bees can continue to pollinate the plants around the rainforest.

WHAT'S YOUR SUPERPOWER?

We can all do our bit to help the environment. Why not try cutting your consumption of plastic packaging, for example, or eating certain foods instead of others? You could walk or cycle instead of using petrol-driven vehicles, and reduce the amount of rubbish you produce by recycling or looking for alternatives. It's not always easy for us to live in a way that doesn't have a negative effect on the world around us, and it's not going to be easy to fix the damage we've collectively caused ... but every little helps and if enough people crave change then anything can be achieved. We can save the planet!